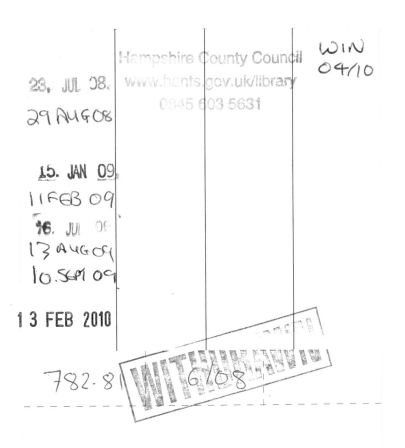

D1334353

C014145861

The Legendary Musicals *of* Boublil & Schönberg

Wise Publications
part of The Music Sales Group
London New York Paris Sydney Copenhagen Berlin Madrid Tokyo

Published by
Wise Publications
14-15 Berners Street, London W1T 3LJ, UK.

Exclusive Distributors:

Music Sales Limited
Distribution Centre, Newmarket Road,
Bury St Edmunds, Suffolk IP33 3YB, UK.

Music Sales Pty Limited
120 Rothschild Avenue, Rosebery,
NSW 2018, Australia.

Order No. AM985369
ISBN 1-84609-506-9
This book © Copyright 2006 Wise Publications,
a division of Music Sales Limited.

Cover design by Chloë Alexander
Photographs courtesy of M Le Poer Trench/Rex Features,
Andrew Milligan (NFL/NAP) Rex Features and Alastair Muir (AMX)/Rex Features
Printed in the EU

The American Dream

Music by Claude-Michel Schönberg
Lyrics by Richard Maltby Jr. & Alain Boublil
Adapted from original French Lyrics by Alain Boublil

Recit.

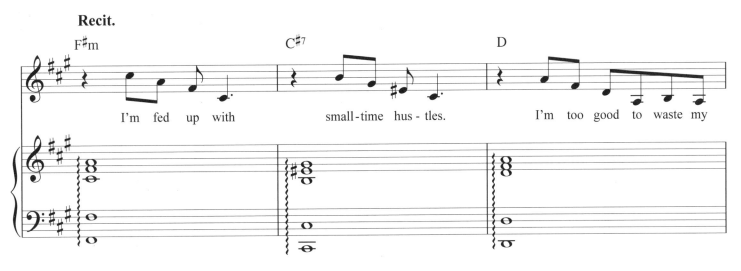

I'm fed up with small-time hus - tles. I'm too good to waste my

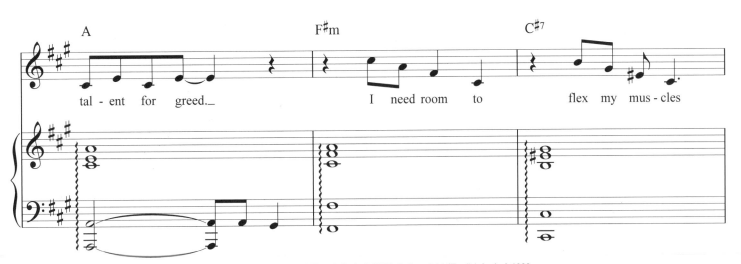

tal - ent for greed.__ I need room to flex my mus - cles

9

-taire, the A - me - ri - can dream.

Schlitz down the drain! Pop the cham- pagne.

It's time we all en - ter -

- tained my A - me - ri - can dream.

At The End Of The Day

Music by Claude-Michel Schönberg
Original Lyrics by Alain Boublil & Jean-Marc Natel
English Lyrics by Herbert Kretzmer

14

Bring Him Home

Music by Claude-Michel Schönberg
Lyrics by Alain Boublil & Herbert Kretzmer

God on high,_____ hear my prayer._____
young._____ He's a - fraid._____
(Verse 2 see block lyric)

In my need You have al -ways been there._____
Let him

He is rest,_____ Hea - ven blessed._____

16

live. _____ Bring him home_____ Bring him

home_____ Bring him home._____

Verse 2
Bring him peace, bring him joy.
He is young, he is only a boy.
You can take it. You can give.
Let him be. Let him live.
If I die, let me die.
Let him live. Bring him home,
Bring him home. Bring him home.

Au Petit Matin

Music & lyrics by Alain Boublil, Raymond Jeannot,
Claude-Michel Schönberg & Jean-Max Rivière

en - tre les mains___ de Dieu._____ Je vous

ai - me,   a - dieu,   a - dieu.   3. Au pe - tit ma -

4. Le pe - tit ma - tin,   n'est dé -

-jà   plus très   loin.   La der - nière é - toile

Verse 3:
Au petit matin
Mes rêves je m'en souviens emportaient mon coeur
Au temps de mon enfance parmi des gens heureux
Un compagnon de jeu, un soir, a pleuré mon départ.

21

A Bas Tous Les Privilèges

Music & Lyrics by Alain Boublil, Raymond Jeannot,
Claude-Michel Schönberg & Jean-Max Rivière

1. Av - ec   de la poudre aux yeux,__   vous av - ez cru fin - ir la

ré - vo - lu - tion._____ C'ét - ait ou - bli - er un peu___ nos am -

-bi - tions.

2. L'é - ga - li - té   ça
3. L'im - pôt d'E - glise   moi

C7

na suf - fit pas,___   en - core faut - il l'ap - pli - quer de - vant la loi.___
j'en fais re - mise,___   mon droit de chasse je l'a - ban - donne à la mas - se.

A - lors___   si vous vou - lez bien,___ al - lons plus loin.
Et puis___   la pen - sion du roi,___ sup - pri - mons - la!

Bethlehem

Music by Claude-Michel Schönberg
Lyrics by Alain Boublil, Edward Hardy & Stephen Clark

29

Bui-Doi

Music by Claude-Michel Schönberg
Lyrics by Richard Maltby Jr. & Alain Boublil
Adapted from original French Lyrics by Alain Boublil

Like all__ sur - vi - vors__ I once thought when I'm home I won't give a damn,__ but now I know I'm caught I'll nev - er leave Vi - et - nam.

These kids__ hit walls on ev-'ry side, they don't be - long in a - ny place.__ Their se - cret they can't hide, it's print - ed on their face.

living reminders of all the good we failed to do. That's why we
fathers and a family, a loving home they never knew. Because we

know, deep in out hearts,___ that they're all our children too.

1.

2.

These are souls in need, they need us to give.

Some-one has to pay for their chance to live. They're called Bui-

Castle On A Cloud

Music by Claude-Michel Schönberg
Original Lyrics by Alain Boublil & Jean-Marc Natel
English Lyrics by Herbert Kretzmer

Charles Gauthier

Music & Lyrics by Alain Boublil, Raymond Jeannot,
Claude-Michel Schönberg & Jean-Max Rivière

Chouans, En Avant!

Music & Lyrics by Alain Boublil, Raymond Jeannot,
Claude-Michel Schönberg & Jean-Max Rivière

42

Do You Hear The People Sing?

Music by Claude-Michel Schönberg
Original Lyrics by Alain Boublil & Jean-Marc Natel
English Lyrics by Herbert Kretzmer

44

mu - sic of a peo - ple Who will not be slaves a - gain! When the

bea - ting of your heart Echoes the bea - ting of the drums, There is a life a - bout to start When to-mor - row

comes! Will you comes.

Drink With Me

Music by Claude-Michel Schönberg
Lyrics by Alain Boublil & Herbert Kretzmer

The Fall Of Saigon

Music by Claude-Michel Schönberg
Lyrics by Alain Boublil & Richard Maltby Jr.
Adapted from Original Lyrics by Alain Boublil

Sor-ry, ser-geant, we must ac - ce-ler-ate; state de-part-ment says we e - va-cu-ate. The

word is we__ must be out by dawn. Sor-ry, ser-geant, it's straight from Wash-ing-ton:

no - one leaves the grounds now, not a - ny - one. As fast as we__ load the planes, we're

gone. (But my girl's out there.)   O. K!__ Keep qui - et don't shout,__ the Am -

-bas - sa - dor won't leave till ev - 'ry - one's out. The chop - per's on the way there's room__ for you all.

52

A Heart Full Of Love

Music by Claude-Michel Schönberg
Original Lyrics by Alain Boublil & Jean-Marc Natel
English Lyrics by Herbert Kretzmer

selle, I am lost in your spell. A heart full _____ of love! A heart full _____ of you! The words are fool-ish but they're true: Cos-ette! Cos-ette! Or were we dream - ing when we met? Who can say? Who can tell? A

54

Empty Chairs At Empty Tables

Music by Claude-Michel Schönberg
Lyrics by Alain Boublil & Herbert Kretzmer

Français, Français

Music & Lyrics by Alain Boublil, Raymond Jeannot,
Claude-Michel Schönberg & Jean-Max Rivière

Here Comes The Morning

Music by Claude-Michel Schönberg

Lyrics by Alan Boublil, Stephen Clark, Edward Hardy & Herbert Kretzmer

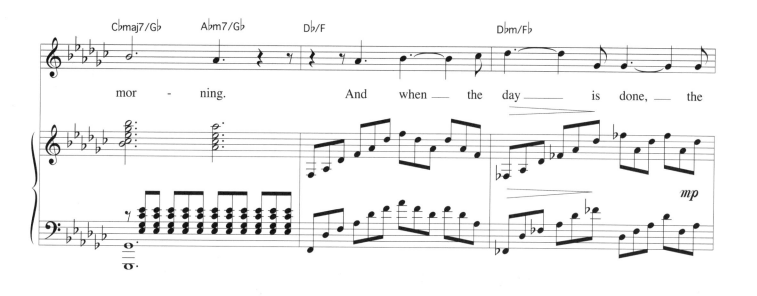

mor - ning. And when — the day — is done, — the

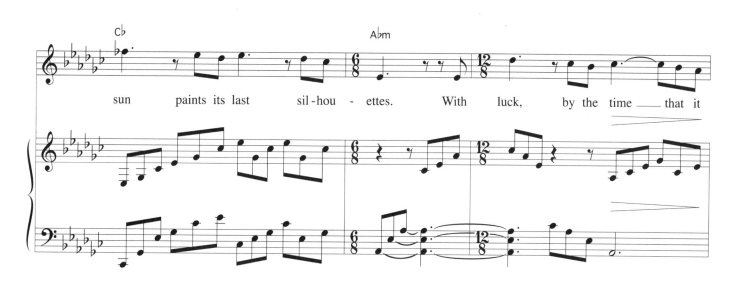

sun paints its last sil-hou - ettes. With luck, by the time — that it

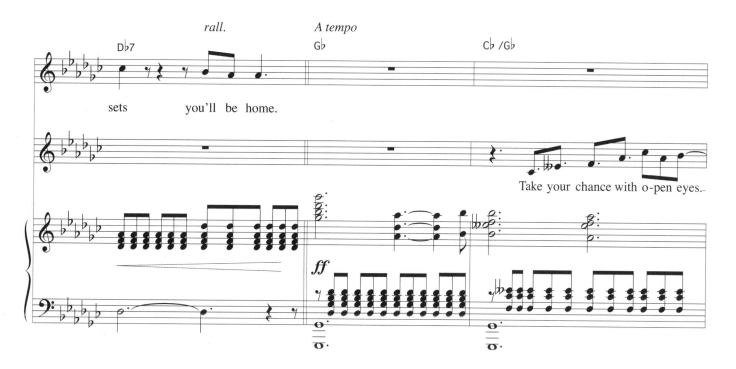

sets you'll be home.

Take your chance with o-pen eyes.

The Land Of The Fathers

Music by Claude-Michel Schönberg
Lyrics by Alain Boublil, Edward Hardy & Stephen Clark

For the deeds that were done in the name of our Lord,

for the deeds that were done in the name of our land,

for the deeds___ that were done___ in the name of the truth,

God have mer-cy on us.

All the false-hoods we prized,

or the vows___ we be-trayed;

for the men we des-pised,

for the price that they paid,

but we hope and we pray for Spring.

May your jour - ney be safe, may your child be strong,

and one day I pray you'll re - turn to your land.

But the grief would re - main and the sor - row would grow.

How Many Tears?

Music by Claude-Michel Schönberg
Lyrics by Alain Boublil & Stephen Clark

candle in his name.

How many tears though the years can I cry? How many prayers to the Lord must I

try? Still the pain tears at my broken heart. Sometimes I feel I was cursed from the start.

All I could hold, all I could see, so full of promise,

80

I Dreamed A Dream

Music by Claude-Michel Schönberg
Original Lyrics by Alain Boublil & Jean-Marc Natel
English Lyrics by Herbert Kretzmer

I dreamed that God would be for - giv - ing.
No song un - sung, no wine un - tast - ed.

But the ti-gers come at night,
With their voi-ces soft as thun - der;

As they tear your hope a - part,
As they turn your dream to shame.

3. He slept a sum-mer by my side,

I'd Give My Life For You

Music by Claude-Michel Schönberg
Lyrics by Richard Maltby Jr. & Alain Boublil
Adapted from original French Lyrics by Alain Boublil

and you should know it's love that brought you here.___ And in one per-fect night, when the stars burned like new I knew what I must do. I'll give you___ a mil-lion things I'll nev-er own. I'll give you___ a world to con-quer when you're grown.

but there's just moon-light on my bed.

Was he a ghost, was he a lie___

that made my bo-dy laugh and cry?___

Then by my side the proof I see,___

his lit-tle one. Gods of the sun___

bring him to me.

You will be who you want to be. You

La Fête de l'Etre Suprême

Music & Lyrics by Alain Boublil, Raymond Jeannot,
Claude-Michel Schönberg & Jean-Max Rivière

94

La Terreur Est En Nous

**Music & Lyrics by Alain Boublil, Raymond Jeannot,
Claude-Michel Schönberg & Jean-Max Rivière**

vo - lu - tion.

Ou ta belle gueule ar - is - to - cra - tique.

Se pro - mèn-'ra au bout d'un-e pique,__ la ter-reur est en nous.__

D.S. al Coda

Coda

The Last Night Of The World

Music by Claude-Michel Schönberg
Lyrics by Richard Maltby Jr. & Alain Boublil
Adapted from original French Lyrics by Alain Boublil

CHRIS

In a place that won't let us feel,

in a place where no-thing seems real,

I have found you.

101

hearts drown the dis-tant drums,_____ and we have mu-sic al-right_

rit.

BOTH

tear-ing the night._ A song, played on a

so - lo sax - o - phone,___ a cra - zy sound._

CHRIS

A

KIM

A lone - ly sound,_ a

cry that tells us love___ goes on and on.___ Played on a

so - lo sax - o - phone.___ It's tell - ing me___ to hold you tight___ and

dance, like it's the last___ night of the world.

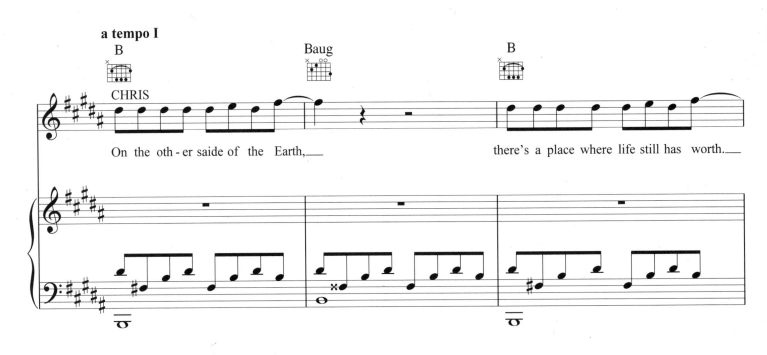

So stay with me___ and hold me tight___ and dance, like it's the

last night of the world.___

L'Exil

Music & Lyrics by Alain Boublil, Raymond Jeannot,
Claude-Michel Schönberg & Jean-Max Rivière

cè - re.
Les au - rons-nous en-sem - ble sur la

ter - re.

Qua-tre sai-sons c'est pour - tant peu de cho - se.

C'est un ma - tin dans la vie d'u - - ne

111

Little People

Music by Claude-Michel Schönberg
Original Lyrics by Alain Boublil & Jean-Marc Natel
English Lyrics by Herbert Kretzmer

won't give up. So you'd bet-ter run for cov-er when the pup grows up!

faster

Bra - vo lit - tle Ga - vroche, you're the top of the class.___ So

what are we gon - na do with this snake in the grass?___

Tie this man and take him to the ta - vern in there.___ The

116

Live With Somebody You Love

Music by Claude-Michel Schönberg
Lyrics by Alain Boublil & Stephen Clark

Master Of The House

Music by Claude-Michel Schönberg
Original Lyrics by Alain Boublil & Jean-Marc Natel
English Lyrics by Herbert Kretzmer

Glad to do my friends a fa - vour _____ Does-n't cost me to be nice but
Re - si -dents are more than wel - come _____ Bri - dal suite is oc - cu - pied! _____

no - thing gets you no - thing Ev - 'ry -thing has got a lit - tle price! _____
Rea -son - a - ble charg - es Plus _____ some lit - tle ex - tra on the side! _____

Mas - ter of the House Keep-er of the zoo Rea -dy to re - lieve them of a
Charge 'em for the lice Ex - tra for the mice Two per-cent for look-ing in the

sou, or two. Wa -ter -ing the wine Ma -king up the weight Pick-ing up their knick-knacks When they
mir - ror twice! Here a lit - tle slice There a lit - tle cut Three percent for sleep - ing with the

can't see straight
Eve - ry - bo - dy loves a land - lord ____
Eve - ry - bo - dy's bo - som friend _
win-dow shut!
When it comes to fix - ing pri - ces ____
There are lots of tricks he knows _

On repeat only

I
How it all in - crea - ses All ____ them bits and pie - ces Je -

1st time only

do what - ev - er plea - ses Je - sus! don't I bleed 'em in the end!
- sus! It's a - maz - ing how it grows!

CHORUS

Ma - ster of the House   Quick to catch yer eye   Ne - ver wants a pass - er by To   pass him by.

Ser-vant to the poor Butler to the great Com-for-ter, phil-os-o-pher And

life-long mate! Eve-ry-bo-dy's boon com-pan-ion ____

Eve-ry-bo-dy's cha-pe-rone. ____ But lock up your va-li-ses Je-
Gives 'em eve-ry-thing he's got. ____ Dir-ty bunch of gee-zers Je-

-sus! Won't I skin yer to the bone!
-sus! What a sor-ry lit-tle lot!

Now That I've Seen Her

Music by Claude-Michel Schönberg
Lyrics by Richard Maltby Jr. & Alain Boublil
Adapted from original French Lyrics by Alain Boublil

Moderato

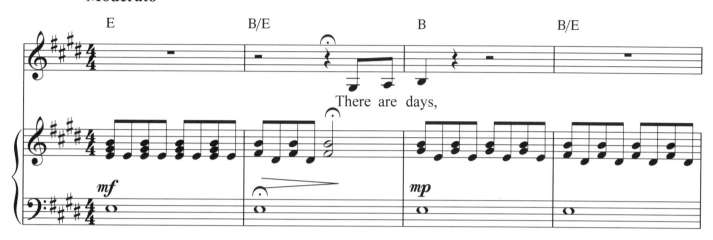

There are days,

there are days when your life clouds ov - er, and the

world gets_ so dark that all at once you can't tell night from

131

135

The Movie In My Mind

Music by Claude-Michel Schönberg
Lyrics by Richard Maltby Jr. & Alain Boublil
Adapted from original French Lyrics by Alain Boublil

137

138

139

On My Own

Music by Claude-Michel Schönberg
Original Lyrics by Alain Boublil & Jean-Marc Natel
English Lyrics by Herbert Kretzmer, Trevor Nunn & John Caird

And now I'm all a - lone a - gain; no - where to go, no one to turn to.

Sun And Moon

Music by Claude-Michel Schönberg
Lyrics by Richard Maltby Jr. & Alain Boublil
Adapted from original French Lyrics by Alain Boublil

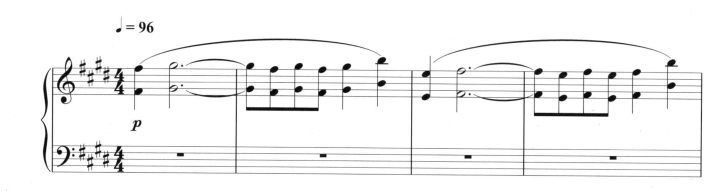

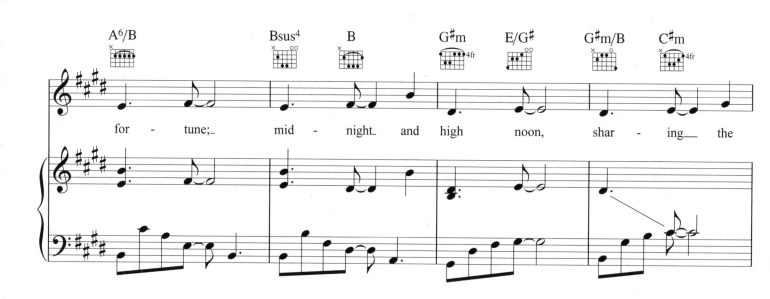

148

Why God Why?

Music by Claude-Michel Schönberg
Lyrics by Richard Maltby Jr. & Alain Boublil
Adapted from original French Lyrics by Alain Boublil